# Extremely WEIRD

## BIRDS

**Text by Sarah Lovett**

**John Muir Publications**
**Santa Fe, New Mexico**

**SPECIAL THANKS to Bill Aragon, Curator of Birds, Rio Grande Zoo**

John Muir Publications, P.O. Box 613, Santa Fe, NM 87504
Copyright © 1992 by John Muir Publications
All rights reserved.
Printed in the United States of America

**Second edition. First printing August 1996**

Library of Congress Cataloging-in-Publication Data
Lovett, Sarah, 1953–
    Birds / text by Sarah Lovett;
[illustrations, Mary Sundstrom, Beth Evans]. — 2nd ed.
        p.    cm. — (Extremely weird)
    Includes index.
    Summary: Describes interesting birds such as the flightless single wattled cassowary; the
brown pelican, whose beak holds more than its belly; the graceful swimmer, the hoatzin,
and others.
    ISBN 1-56261-279-4  (pbk.)
    1. Exotic birds—Juvenile literature. [1. Birds.]    I. Sundstrom, Mary, ill.
II. Evans, Beth, ill.    III. Title.    IV. Series: Lovett, Sarah, 1953–  Extremely weird
QL676.2.L68    1996
598—dc20                                          96-14769
                                                    CIP
                                                    AC

Extremely Weird Logo Art: Peter Aschwanden
Illustrations: Mary Sundstrom, Beth Evans
Design: Sally Blakemore
Printer: Guynes Lithographers

Distributed to the book trade by
Publishers Group West
Emeryville, California

**Cover photo: KING VULTURE (*Sarcoramphus papa*)**
**Cover photo courtesy Photo Researchers, Inc.**

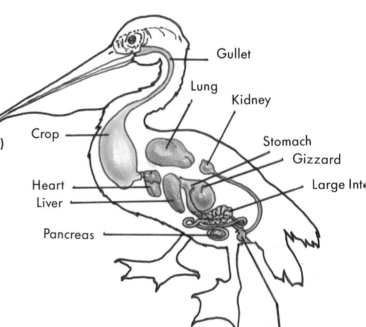

Gullet

Lung

Kidney

Crop

Stomach

Gizzard

Large Int

Heart

Liver

Pancreas

Cloaca, the cavity where the inte
and urinary tracts end

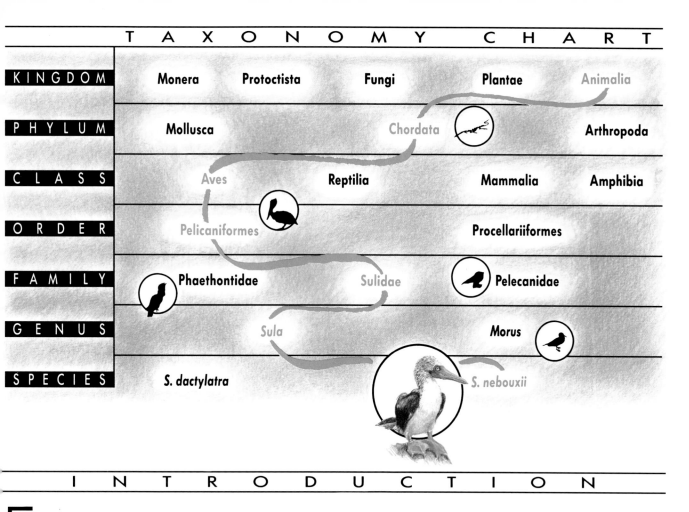

# TAXONOMY CHART

| | | | | | |
|---|---|---|---|---|---|
| **KINGDOM** | Monera | Protoctista | Fungi | Plantae | Animalia |
| **PHYLUM** | Mollusca | | Chordata | | Arthropoda |
| **CLASS** | Aves | Reptilia | | Mammalia | Amphibia |
| **ORDER** | Pelicaniformes | | | Procellariiformes | |
| **FAMILY** | Phaethontidae | Sulidae | | Pelecanidae | |
| **GENUS** | Sula | | | Morus | |
| **SPECIES** | S. dactylatra | | | S. nebouxii | |

# INTRODUCTION

Eagles soar, hummingbirds hover, gulls glide, and swifts flap. Soaring, hovering, gliding, and flapping are four ways that birds navigate the air currents. Many birds use all four kinds of flight, but each bird has its own specialty. Out of more than 8,600 bird species in the world, less than 50 species are flightless.

Birds have become masters of flight since their reptilian ancestors first glided over prehistoric swamps 200 million years ago. Birds and bats are the only vertebrate animals capable of muscle-powered flight. What makes birds so special? Feathers. All birds have two legs and two feet and lungs to breathe oxygen, but so do many animals. And birds hatch out of hard-shelled eggs, but eggs don't fly. And although birds certainly are not the only creatures with wings, they *are* the world's only feathered animals. Feathers help maintain a bird's internal body temperature. And they also aid flight: feathers increase the streamlined shape of a bird's body and give wings the airfoil shape that human engineers copy when they design airplanes.

Airplanes are mostly lifted off the ground by a passive process: the shape of the wing causes a difference in air pressure. Because air pressure is lower above the wing and higher below, planes rise. The same ideas apply when birds like storks and vultures soar. To soar, birds spread their wings and hitch a ride on an updraft of warm air. Flapping bird flight, in contrast, is an active process whereby birds use their muscles to flap their wings and push against the air. Hovering flight (used by small birds like sparrows, finches, and hummingbirds) takes a lot of energy! Wings are moved so quickly back and forth that the bird's body stays upright. Gliding flight is really a long, slow fall that doesn't require much energy.

To fly, it's important to be a lightweight. (Scientists believe it's almost impossible for a bird weighing more than 40 pounds to fly.) Through evolution, birds have lost bones that were not absolutely necessary. And they acquired hollow bones and light horny bills that help them fly light. Most birds have a keeled sternum—it bows out like the keel of a boat—so there is plenty of room for large flight muscles to attach.

To keep track of birds and the millions of animal and plant species on Earth, scientists use a universal system called taxonomy. Taxonomy starts with the five main groups of all living things, the kingdoms, and then divides those into the next group down, the phylum, then class, order, family, genus, and finally, species. Members of a *species* look similar, and they can reproduce with each other. For an example of how taxonomy works, look at the highlighted lines above to see how the blue-footed booby is classified.

As you learn about the birds in this book, look for the scientific name in parentheses after the common name. The first word is the genus; the second word is the species.

Turn to the *glossarized index* at the back of this book if you're looking for a specific bird, or for special information (what's molting, for instance), or for the definition of a word you don't understand.

### ATLANTIC PUFFIN (*Fratercula arctica*)

What stands ten inches tall, has a large red bill, red feet and legs, and holes in its head? What else but an Atlantic puffin!

Atlantic puffins are shorebirds and relatives of auks, dovekies, and murres. True to their name, puffins live along the North Atlantic coast and feed on fish. They mate during the spring. Afterward, they shed the surface of their brightly colored bill.

MARY SUNDSTROM

Because birds don't have teeth, their food is broken down during digestion. Plant-eating birds depend on a small muscular organ called the gizzard to grind up food. The gizzard is often aided by small stones that the bird swallows.

Like other birds, a puffin's skull is full of holes. In fact, many of the bones of a bird's skeleton are hollow. Holey, hollow bones are lighter, and they make it easier for birds to balance. Of course, bird bones must be strong as well as light. Bones that are tube-shaped (like straws) have thin, crosswise supports inside, resembling honeycomb. Other bones contain air sacs that are connected to the lungs. These "balloons" make birds even lighter and increase oxygen flow. Another plus: birds like the Atlantic puffin are equipped with bills instead of teeth. Bird bills are horny (not bony), and they weigh grams instead of kilograms. If you're always on the ground, like humans, elephants, and horses, you can afford a heavy skeleton, but fliers must be lightweights, or featherweights!

MARY LAMBERT

A puffin "flies" underwater, turns its head from side to side, and picks fish from a school until its beak is filled to capacity!

Owls are so flexible, they can look at the world with an upside-down head!

### ORIENTAL BAY OWL (*Phodilus badius*)

Owls are carnivores, which means they eat other animals such as spiders, insects, crustaceans, fish, frogs, rodents, and birds. Since most owls are nocturnal (night) hunters, nature has provided some fancy equipment for locating prey after dark. Owl eyes and sockets are big, and the owl's eyesight is keen. But they depend most on excellent hearing for their hunting edge. The disk-like shape of the owl's face—enhanced by hard, wiry feathers—helps direct sound. The disk serves the same function as the external earflaps of most mammals. Other birds only have ear holes.

Owls also depend on silence and surprise to ensure a successful hunt. Their flight feathers are set in a loose weave and fringed with special barbs or "sound dampers" for silent attacks on unsuspecting prey. These powerful hunters have strong legs and sharp curved talons (claws) that make it possible to grasp their prey.

Most small and medium-sized owls nest in trees. They sometimes choose holes excavated by woodpeckers or other animals. Larger owls may build nests of grass, feathers, and twigs or borrow stick nests abandoned by hawks, crows, and other birds. In most species, the male is responsible for feeding his mate and offspring from the time incubation begins until the young fledge. Often, the female is much larger than the male.

Oriental bay owls live in parts of northern India, Sri Lanka, and Southeast Asia. Adults are almost 12 inches (29 cm) tall and feed mostly on insects. They raise three to five young in their nests built in tree hollows.

Some burrowing owls use the spare tunnels of the predatory badger for raising their young. Manure, packed into the burrow by the bird, probably keeps the badger from smelling the nest.

Head backward! An owl's eyes are positioned on the front of its face, like a human's eyes. For this reason, owls can't see to the side as easily as other birds. Not without turning their heads, that is. Owls can move their heads in half circles in either direction so they look as if they're on backward!

BIRDS

## ANDEAN CONDOR (*Vultur gryphus*)

Eons ago, when California condors roamed what is now the American West, they devoured the rotting flesh of saber-toothed tigers and mastodons.

Wings spanning 10 feet, a gray and wrinkled naked head and neck, and claws the size of human hands make the Andean condor an imposing sight. It is one of the largest flying birds in the world and can reach an air speed of 60 miles per hour and travel 140 miles per day in search of food. It lives mostly in the Andes, from Venezuela to Patagonia, in South America.

Andean condors are vultures, birds of prey that are active in the daytime. Like all vultures, they have naked heads and nostrils that look like holes that have been drilled through their large bill. They feed exclusively on carrion (dead flesh), which they locate by smell.

The Andean condor is an endangered species. There are many reasons modern life has proved deadly to these birds. They have been killed by hunters, head-on collisions with power lines, and poison. Fossil records show that condors date back at least 100,000 years and that they once devoured the flesh of mammoths and saber-tooth tigers. Now, they struggle to survive.

The California condor, a close relative of the Andean condor, is another extremely rare bird. Only a century ago, they nested in caves and rocky crevices in cliffs along the Pacific coast of California. By 1980, there were so few California condors surviving in the wild, they were captured and moved to sanctuaries. Captive breeding programs have increased their numbers, and plans for reintroduction to natural habitats are under way. Only time will tell if this endangered bird will fly wild once again.

Clean bones! In only twenty minutes, a flock of vultures can pick a deer's bones clean.

Almost all birds have two types of vision—binocular and monocular. Unlike humans, birds' eyes are not set on the front of their face (except raptors) but on each side of their head. Each eye has its own field of vision, and when the two monocular fields overlap to form a single image, birds have binocular vision. The woodcock's eyes are set so far to the side, it can actually see in a complete circle without turning its head!

BIRDS

### SINGLE-WATTLED CASSOWARY (*Casuarius unappendiculatis*)

Birds fly. At least most of them do. But there are some birds who spend all their time on the ground. Flightless birds can be divided into two groups: those whose ancestors flew at one time (penguins, for example) and those whose ancestors probably never flew (such as the cassowary).

Since the ancestors of some birds may have given up flight millions of years ago, how does anybody know for sure who flew and who didn't? Ornithologists (people who study birds) know that most birds have a keel-shaped sternum (breastbone) that juts out like the bottom of a boat. This shape means there is lots of room for large flight muscles to attach to the bone. Although penguins are flightless, their sternum *is* keeled, and their wing stroke under water is mechanically identical to an aerial wing stroke. Flightless cassowaries, in contrast, have flat sternums. In fact, cassowaries are also known as "ratites," which means raftlike, or flat.

Huge single-wattled cassowaries grow to a height of 5 feet, and they can run at 30 miles per hour, leap, and swim, but they can't get off the ground. Not with their wings, that is. Cassowaries use their smallish wings to ward off sticks and branches when they sprint through the forests of New Guinea and Australia, where they live. They eat fruits, insects, and plants. Because they're grounded, cassowaries defend themselves with long, slashing, razorlike nails on their inner toes.

The female cassowary deposits four or five giant, green eggs on a nest of leaves at the foot of a tree. From then on, her mate must incubate, brood, feed, and care for the young.

What's a wattle? That weird, fleshy, wrinkly, often brightly colored flap of skin that adorns the faces of certain birds such as the cassowary.

The ostrich (another ratite) is the world's biggest living bird! Eight feet tall from head to both toes, the adult ostrich can race along at 40 (even 45!) miles per hour.

Moas are extinct birds that looked like pin-headed ostriches. These giants could reach a height of 12 feet and weighed more than 500 pounds. Moas used to live in New Zealand.

# B I R D S

## BROWN PELICAN (*Pelecanus occidentalis*)

The pelican is known for its enormous beak that holds more than its belly can. Actually, the lower beak has an expandable skin pouch, which is filled and filled and filled with fish. White pelicans dine on freshwater fish from marshes, lagoons, and lakes. Brown pelicans, in contrast, feed only in salt water. They have developed a special skill for fishing.

The brown pelican is a high-diver extraordinaire. From a height of 20 meters (more than 60 feet) or less, it plunges straight downward or in a spiral, with its head close to its body and wings partly folded, to strike the water head first and disappear. Then, after pouch-netting fish, it pops up again like a bobbing cork.

Although they are aerial acrobats, swooping, gliding, and floating on the air currents, pelicans have trouble when it comes to takeoffs. They're not really heavy, but they are large. They solve the problem of size by running full-speed-ahead, webbed paddle feet slapping the water's surface.

Brown pelicans spend their lives on both coasts of North America and the west coast of South America. In crowded, busy colonies they breed and nest on islands where there are few predators. Although mature pelicans can be noisy—they hiss, blow, groan, and sometimes clatter their beaks together—the young *really* create a din. Barking, squeaking, bleating, grunting, and groaning are all part of a young pelican's vocabulary.

White pelicans team up to catch fish! Forming a line, pelicans paddle forward, driving fish to shallow waters where they are easily pouched up.

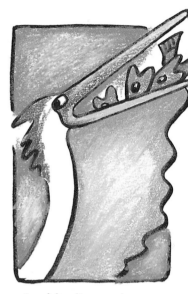

An adult pelican can devour more than 10 pounds of fish per day!

A pelican parent's bill may be five times as long as its newly hatched youngster. And an adult pelican's wing can span 9 feet!

Anhingas, or "snake-birds," have sharp beaks made for spearing fish. When the anhinga tosses its meal overhead, it can catch it with open beak, just like you catch peanuts!

## SOUTHERN BALD IBIS (*Geronticus calvus*)

Ibises, like storks, flamingos, herons, and jabirus, are long-legged waders. These birds live in colonies in most marshy tropical areas of the world. Their long, narrow beaks curve downward and are handy for picking insects, crabs, mollusks, and worms from mud and dirt. Sometimes, ibises catch larger prey such as frogs and small rodents. These quick critters have even been known to snap hummingbirds from midair.

In flight, ibises alternate wing strokes with gliding movements, and all birds in a flock seem to make their moves together.

Generally, the ibis has sturdy legs of medium length (about 12 inches), and its neck and face are bare of feathers. The southern bald ibis lives in parts of South Africa. Its relative, the northern bald ibis, lives in North Africa and Europe. Other species include the sacred ibis, scarlet ibis, hermit ibis, and wattled ibis.

The ostrich has two large toes on each foot, and these are handy for dashing across soft African sand. Scientists believe that eventually, the ostrich might have only one toe, just like a horse! That's a foot of evolution for you!

Flying dino! A bird's keeled breastbone is made to attach flight muscles. Its shoulder joints are made for flapping. Otherwise, some dinosaur skeletons and the skeletons of the first flying birds aren't all that different. Both had tails, and both had air sacs to lighten their bodies.

## JABIRU STORK (*Jabiru mycteria*)

Spindly-legged, knobby-kneed, long-billed storks don't look like lucky birds, but in fairy tales and folklore, that's just what they are. Because some species live near towns, villages, and people, storks have starred in many tall tales. Storks are said to bring good fortune and prosperity. Although storks don't really deliver newborn babies to happy parents, many of these birds appear big enough for the job.

The jabiru, which lives in the area extending from Argentina to Mexico, is the largest stork— and one of the largest flying birds—in the New World. Jabirus grow to lengths of more than four and a half feet. When airborne, the jabiru stretches its body from neck to toes, and wing-flapping alternates with gliding as a method of flight.

Besides the jabiru, there are 16 known species of storks, and they live mostly in tropical marshes and swamps. European white storks are an exception. They spend some of the year in parts of Europe and then migrate to warmer areas. Storks are omnivorous: they eat plants and small animals such as insects, frogs, and snakes.

Australian Aborigines have a legend that features the kookaburra. At the time of the world's very first sunrise, the god Bayame ordered kookaburra to laugh loudly enough to wake up humankind. Bayame didn't want humans to miss the incredible sight.

The kookaburra is also known as a "bushman's clock" because it laughs promptly at sunrise and sunset in the Australian bush.

Nestlings are baby birds that are dependent on their parents.

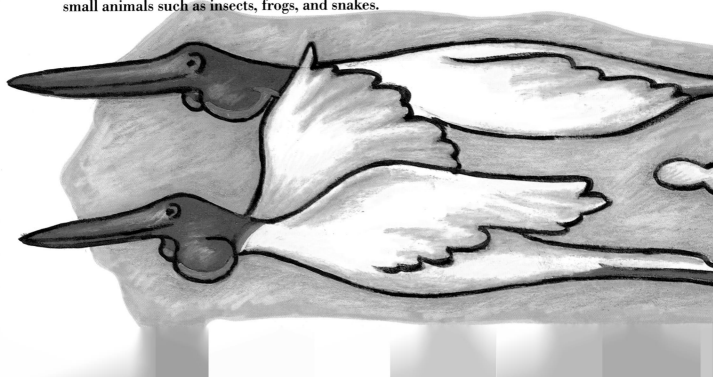

# A Shoe Fit

## SHOEBILL STORK (*Balaeniceps rex*)

One of the weirdest storks of all is the shoe-bill, and if you use your imagination, this stork's thick, high bill does look a bit like unusual footwear. It has also been described as a "whale-headed" stork, and, in fact, that's what its scientific name means. It may even resemble some birds you've seen in cartoons.

Shoebills are found only in the marshlands of tropical Africa where they spend their days near rivers or grassy flood areas. Their bootlike bills—8 inches long and almost as wide—are perfect for probing in muddy water. They eat river fish, frogs, and snails, and they prefer to hunt for food at night. These shy birds are ground nesters, and they usually lay two eggs in flat grassy areas. Like all storks, shoebills are able fliers.

The shoebill stork has a tiny comb built into its central toenail which it uses to "comb" its feathers. Birds do not have oil glands in their skin like humans do. Instead, they have a preen gland located at the base of their tails. They also have powder down (feathers that have turned to powder), which they use with the oil to groom and waterproof their feathers.

Storks are mute because they have no voicebox. Storks clatter their bills to get their point across.

### GROUND HORNBILL (*Bucorvus leadbeateri*)

Boasting a swollen 9-inch-long bill, a frill of long eye-lashes, and a red or blue inflatable throat sac, the ground hornbill is as large and as weird-looking as a turkey. This long-legged bird is the most terrestrial (ground-dwelling) of all the hornbill species. It lives in the savannas of Africa. There, this omnivorous bird hunts for insects, reptiles, mice, and other bird's eggs.

Ground hornbills often nest in hollow trees or cracks and crevices in cliffs, and the female may come and go as she pleases during incubation and rearing of young. That's not the case in most species.

When females of the black dwarf hornbills, rhinoceros hornbills, and others settle down, they are real stay-at-homes. First, a mating hornbill pair chooses a nest site in a tall tree with a hollow cavity. The female lays large white eggs, which she begins to incubate. Eventually, her mate starts to bring home bits of mud and earth, and the female mixes these with bird-droppings and regurgitated food to seal herself inside the nest hole. When the seal is complete, there is only enough room for the tip of her bill to fit through the small opening. This barrier appears to keep predators away from the female and her young, but it leaves the male with a very big job. He must supply food for the female during the 30 to 40 days of incubation. After the young hatch, he may have to feed them all for weeks, even months, until the female feels it's time to escape!

The African jacana is also known as the lily-trotter because it tip-toes over floating lily pads. By spreading its toes, it also spreads out its body weight.

Ornithologists study fossils to understand how different species of birds have evolved or changed over the eons. Archaeopteryx, one of the earliest feathered animals, left a semireptilian print in fossils. It had feathers and could glide but probably spent most of its time on the ground. Was it a bird? Not really. Was it a dinosaur? Probably not. In fact, some scientists believe it may belong to its very own group.

## MADAGASCAR MALACHITE KINGFISHER (*Alcedo cristata vintsioides*)

There are more than 80 known species of kingfishers, and they can be as little as 5 inches or as big as 1½ feet. Kingfishers are divided into two large groups—wood kingfishers and true kingfishers. While wood kingfishers are usually found in forests far from water, true kingfishers spend their active days near streams, rivers, and lakes.

Breeding pairs guard their territory and keep other kingfishers away. They hunt by diving headfirst into water from their hunting perches or from midair like hover-craft. They eat live prey such as fish and water insects.

True kingfishers nest in holes in sandy riverbanks and stream-banks and lake slopes. They use their three fused front toes as scoopers to push out soil already loosened by their long, narrow beak. Some-times, their nests are as deep as one meter (about 3 feet).

When breeding pairs court in the spring, the male brings a gift. He offers his mate a fish, head first (just as the young will be fed). The female lays between six and eight eggs, and when the young hatch, they need tiny fish on their first day of life. Each young kingfisher eats about six fish per day, gulped whole.

Give me a brake! Landing birds lower and fan their tail feathers to use them as air brakes as they approach a perch.

Geese and some other water birds use their webbed feet to run across water for takeoffs and landings.

# Booby Prize

### BLUE-FOOTED BOOBY (*Sula nebouxii*)

**Bubble pack!** Boobies have air sacs under their skin which help cushion them as they high dive into the water.

Big blue feet and a reputation for being easy to catch have earned the blue-footed booby its name. These goose-sized oceangoing birds spend most of their time cruising tropical or subtropical coastal waters, and they hardly ever visit land except to breed. During the mating season in spring, boobies gather in large colonies, often on islands but sometimes on mainland cliffs. Perched breast to breast, courting pairs use their pointed bills to joust or fence. Boobies make their nests out of seaweed and twigs, or they scrape a shallow hole in the ground. Both parents share in child care.

Boobies are relatives of pelicans and cormorants. They fly with ease, and they are some of the most daring sky-divers among all birds. To catch fish, boobies in flight plunge speedily downward (some from a height of 100 meters, or 320 feet), closing their wings just before they strike the water. The force of the dive takes them below the surface of the ocean where they swim using their wings and feet. Blue-footed boobies also use a group hunting system, in which they all dive at once after one gives a whistling signal.

Several other booby species are able hunters. Red-footed boobies hunt for flying fish and squid, and brown boobies chase fish underwater.

**Flying elephants?** Not exactly. Although Madagascar's elephant birds are extinct (that happened about 700 years ago!), some ornithologists believe they weighed as much as half a ton (1,000 pounds!), and their eggs (which have been found in swamps) weighed more than 25 pounds and could hold two gallons of liquid. Elephant bird eggs were bigger than dinosaur eggs!

## GREATER PRAIRIE CHICKEN (*Tympanuchus cupido*)

Known for their courting rituals, greater prairie chickens are said to have inspired many dances of Great Plains Native Americans. Each spring, the male birds return to traditional dancing sites or "booming grounds" to court females. With neck feathers erect and neck sacs inflated like great orange balloons, they strut, shuffle, and make booming noises.

The sharptail grouse, a relative of the prairie chicken, participates in similar courtship dances. Males shuffle and stamp their feet quickly, heads up and tails down. And they all start and stop at once, on a dime.

Many birds have courting rituals, and some even molt (shed) their regular feathers and grow new, showier, spiffier plumes just for the occasion. A courting male works to impress a female of the species so she will choose him as her mate.

Unfortunately, much of the greater prairie chicken's habitat has been developed for farmland. These birds are an endangered species threatened with extinction.

People use birds as symbols. Doves stand for peace, bluebirds mean happiness, eagles are brave, and owls are wise. Has anyone ever called you a bird brain?

A grouse will fly-dive head first into a snowbank to insulate itself from the cold. Think of it as a bird igloo.

Birds are incredible commuters. They can cross continents and seas during migration. Some migrating geese are known to travel 2,000 miles at 35 miles per hour in three days. Ducks are even faster: they cover 1,000 miles per day at 40 miles per hour.

## KORI BUSTARD (*Ardeotis kori*)

Bustards have been around for years—at least 50 million years, in fact! These days, bustards can be found wandering the semidesert plains of Africa, Australia, and Eurasia. Since they are partial to dry, warm climates, bustards in northern areas are migratory, heading south when the weather changes.

Bustards are medium and large birds, and they fly in typical crane fashion, head and neck straight out front, legs and feet trailing behind, and wings beating steadily. They often travel in flocks of a dozen or so, usually 200 or 300 feet above the ground.

Bustards sleep belly to the ground and head tucked between their shoulders. They almost never take a one-legged stance or perch on branches. Although they're strong fliers, they often escape predators on the run. Like cranes, they are omnivores who eat plants, herbs, grass, insects, snails, mice, and lizards. They also devour lots of locusts.

Bustards do *not* molt (the process by which all birds shed old feathers and replace them) all wing feathers at once, so they are still able to fly. Most birds molt on a yearly basis, and some do it twice a year.

Toe lockers. Why don't sleeping birds fall? Birds are equipped with grippy grabbers. Their feet have toes that "lock" in place when they squat on branches, wires, or other perches. The lock happens when muscles in the bird's upper legs pull attached tendons, which in turn tighten and lock their toes.

Feathers, like hairs, wear out, and birds molt or shed their plumes at least once a year, sometimes twice. Feathers are not shed all at once (except for penguins, ducks, and some other water birds). Most birds lose flight and tail feathers in pairs, so they are always able to fly!

# Birds-of-a-Feather

Pheasants fly only when absolutely necessary, but when they're in danger, they explode into flight. Capable of almost vertical flapping takeoffs, pheasants glide when airborne.

## BULWER'S WATTLED PHEASANT (*Lophura bulweri*)

Bright blue, sickle-shaped wattles, a huge fan of white tail feathers, and the sound of rustling leaves are all tell-tale signs that the Bulwer's wattled pheasant is courting. To impress a potential mate, the male of this species goes through changes. Eyes like red Christmas lights, he struts with head lowered and feathers spread so that he looks a bit like a slow-moving satellite dish. As his tail feathers brush against the ground of the Asian forests where he lives, they shake dry leaves.

When it comes to birds-of-a-different-colored-feather, all pheasants tend to be alike—males and females are distinctly different colors. Male pheasants are some of the most spectacularly feathered birds in the avian kingdom, and many have long technicolored tail feathers. Males sport brighter plumage because they have the job of winning the female's attention. The females' duller plumage provides camouflage while she tends the nest.

The brilliant peacock is a pheasant.

Dirty bird! Dust baths are handy when birds want to scour parasites and dirt from feathers.

This glossarized index will help you find specific information about the birds in this book. It will also help you understand the meaning of some of the words that are used.